Teacher's Selection: Anthology of Eighth Grade Poetry

1998 Edition
Volume XXIII

Published by Anthology of Poetry, Inc.

Teacher's Selection:
Anthology of Eighth Grade Poetry©
1998 Edition
Volume XXIII

Printed in the United States of America

Authors responsible for originality
of poems submitted.

The Anthology of Poetry, Inc.
P.O. Box 698 • 307 East Salisbury
Asheboro, NC   27204-0698

ISBN: 1-883931-15-0

Our belief that children live and think in poetic images is again confirmed by the poetry of this edition. If you want to know what is on the minds of our children, poetry is the window. This edition will let you look through that window to a world prose could never describe. To a world painted with wonder, awe and sometimes confusion, with microscopic inspection of subjects that adults hardly notice and with insight into issues adults also struggle with.

The Anthology of Poetry proudly presents to you the hard bound edition of *Teacher's Selection: Anthology of Eighth Grade Poetry*. The poems of this edition are the top honors from eighth grade classrooms from across the United States. Of all entries from each school only a few receive nominations for publication by each eighth grade teacher. And of those nominations only three are selected for publication. Congratulations.

We thank the eighth grade teachers for their participation in this project and, as always, we applaud the poets who shared their gifts.

We look forward to the publication of upcoming editions of *Teacher's Selection: Anthology of Eighth Grade Poetry*.

The Editors

The One True Reason

The crowd is gone, the lights are out.
There is suddenly deafening silence
all around me.
The tempting aroma of hot dogs and popcorn
no longer linger in the air.
The clouds of blue and pink cotton candy
have diminished.
What brings the throngs of excited people,
and the wide-eyed children to this place?
Is it the chanting of the vendors or
the crack of the bat?
Maybe it's the hope of meeting a star.
As I stand here on the field,
lucky enough to be living my childhood dreams,
I can only guess the one true reason
why they come here.
They come here for the same reason as I do,
for the love of the game, the game of baseball.

Steve Linder

Immaculate Conception
Morris, IL
Nominated by eighth grade teacher Loreen Vlk

The Music

The music,
I feel it all around me,
surrounding me,
filling me with joy.

The music,
it makes me feel whole.
Lost would I be without it,
without its hypnotic voices.

The music,
my source of peace.
A flood of emotions,
it washes over me.

The music,
my refuge, my life,
my key to happiness,
this gift from God.

Anne Jillian Yatco

Immaculate Conception
Morris, IL
Nominated by eighth grade teacher Loreen Vlk

Love

Love is complicated or so I hear;
You may even shed a tear.

Love can make you sad,
But is not all that bad.

Love can be a blessing,
Or so I am guessing.

Love is your life,
With a husband or a wife.

Love will be your friend;
Your troubles it will mend.

Love is forever,
With whomever,

You can share,
The things you hold dear.

Candice Zielinski

St Gerald
Oak Lawn, IL
Nominated by eighth grade teacher
Mrs. Maureen Thompson

A Dreamer's Oasis

If someone were to ask me,
"How do you prefer to move?"
And I replied, " By walking,"
I'm sure that he'd approve.

But if I were to answer,
"By the fingers on my hands,"
I don't think he'd be able
To completely understand.

Together, my precious fingers
Can take me everywhere,
From Spain and France to Mexico,
If I had to travel there.

You see, these special fingers
Entertain with incredible songs,

That can take a person anywhere,
Like a palace in Hong Kong.

"How can that be?" one skeptically thinks.
"Only vehicles take you to those places!"
But nothing can stop the power of the mind,
As my piano is a dreamer's oasis.

Meena Babu

St Gerald
Oak Lawn, IL
Nominated by eighth grade teacher
Mrs. Maureen Thompson

A Big Dream For A Little Girl

One day she wanted something new to do,
but never thought this game
would turn into a dream that came true.
She knew what games girls and boys played,
but she wanted it anyway.
She never thought she'd be in the spotlight,
she just wanted it for the fight.
She had desire and speed.
What else does a hockey player need?
She was the best on her team,
but the scouts didn't care she had a dream.
She always wanted to know why
the girls weren't chosen over the guys?
Then tears would always come to her eyes.
The answer she always heard was,
"It's because you're a girl,
and they don't think you can play."
But maybe it will all happen, someday.......

Jill Harper

St. Louis de Montfast
Oak Lawn, IL
Nominated by eighth grade teacher Bonnie McGinnis

Love

Love can be between a parent and child,
Showing that they always care.
Love can make one feel special,
By showing affection anywhere.
Love can mean taking the time
To do all we can,
By giving everything to others
And lending a helpful hand.

Love can bring out the best in us,
And help us get through good times and bad.
Love can bring out inner beauty,
And show us the good things we have.

True love can be unconditional,
But only you can make love happen.

Katie Lynn Wojtanowicz

St. Louis de Montfast
Oak Lawn, IL
Nominated by eighth grade teacher Bonnie McGinnis

Two

Two is a number that says many things.
With two there is always more than one
Which means twice the fun!
You could do a duet instead of a solo.
Two.
Two is a couple.
Two is a pair.
Two hands, two feet, two eyes, two ears.
And two barrettes in my hair.
Two.
Two is less than a few.
And more than one or none.
It falls between uno and tres.
It's dos!
Two.
Two is for February.
Two is for 2:00.
Two hours, two days, two weeks, two months.
Two more years until 2000!
Two.

Lauren Jesse

St Gerald
Oak Lawn, IL
Nominated by eighth grade teacher Mrs. Maureen
Thompson

The Mask

She wears a mask.
It hides her true self.
Hiding her feelings deep inside her.
She wears the mask quite well.
Afraid without it someone might figure her out.
Yet she yearns for someone to understand her.
For someone to reach out to her.
Someone to give a care about her.
Yet she doesn't remove the mask.
She lives a secret life.
A life filled with pain and sadness.
You will find this life deep inside her heart.
But her mask hides this well.
Her mask only shows happiness and joy.
She dare not let her true self show.
Her mask is not only a mask
But now it is her personality.
A mask.
A simple thing but oh how it has changed her life.

Christina DeOrnellas

St. George
Tinley Park, IL
Nominated by eighth grade teacher M. Pries

Nugget

She's the best dog in the whole world
She plays with me when I'm sad and I never get bored
She's always friendly and loves to lick
Even when she is sick
Her favorite game is tug-of-war
Even though I think it's a bore
She's always happy and never sad
She makes everybody feel glad
She welcomes people to our house
Even though she is about the same size as a mouse
I'm glad we have her and hope we never part
Because she'll always be with me in my heart.

Katie Tannheimer

St. George
Tinley Park, IL
Nominated by eighth grade teacher M. Pries

A Homeless Child

Child, child, what are you thinking?
Child, child, what have you been drinking?
Child, child, sleeping in the cold,
Child, child, "This is life," is that what you're told?
Child, child, thin and starving,
Rich people sit, a lovely turkey they are carving.

Child, child, you don't have a pet,
Child, child, bags of garbage down you set.
Child, child, you don't sleep in a bed,
Child, child, a cardboard box
Is where you rest your head.
Child, child, you feel very sad,
Child, child, you're not even bad,
Child, child, God will still love you,
Even if people push and shove you.

Kathleen Shifley

St. Francis Xavier School
LaGrange, IL
Nominated by eighth grade teacher Denise Salemi

Walk On The Beach

I walk hand in hand
with my father at three.
He's tense about something
but enjoys the beach.

I walk hand in hand
with my boyfriend at seventeen.
He's nervous, his hand
squeezes tight around mine.
He does not want
to lose me.

I walk hand in hand
with my husband at twenty-four.
He looks in my eyes.
He thinks I'm
beautiful.
He's trying to tell me something.

I walk hand in hand
with my son at thirty-two.
My son looks up at me.

I'm tense, but I enjoy the beach.
I'm nervous, I squeeze
my hand tight around his.
I do not want to lose him.

I look in his eyes
and see he's beautiful.
I know one day
my son will take
his daughter to the beach
and he will walk hand in hand
with his daughter.

Emilee Frost

Hinsdale Middle School
Hinsdale, IL
Nominated by eighth grade teacher Donna Vorreyer

The Old Abandoned Town

In the old abandoned town,
There was a faint feeling of loss,
Wanting, need, and hopelessness.
When the dust of the old town arose
With the cool gentle wind,
It told a story of when the old town
Was young and beautiful.
When children ran and played,
And picked lovely flowers
In the fertile, green meadows.
When the people talked of wonderful times
That they had shared.
When farmers were harvesting the plentiful fields
Of yellow and gold.
A story was told of when the town
Was loved and not alone.
When people called the old town home.

Tracy Mulick

St. Raphael
Naperville, IL
Nominated by eighth grade teacher Charlene Paprockas

What Is Love??

Let me tell you about love.
It is like a lonesome dove
in the barren night
who flies without a fright.
He's lost in a grateful bliss
remembering his first kiss.
But he knows
that he always shows
his affection for her.
He is blinded by the blur
of knowing he's in love.
"But he is just a dove."
Shall we restrict ourselves to this thought?
When we know what is brought
upon to us by this feeling
which is but always appealing.
This is true love!!
And it is even felt, by a lonesome dove.

Dan Czulno

Timber Ridge Middle School
Plainfield, IL
Nominated by eighth grade teacher Tiffany Kolliopoulos

The Lazy Summer Days

Fresh and full of life,
children playing in the cool spray of a hose,
and parents shouting to their kids
to look both ways before crossing.

There were summer picnics beneath the shady trees,
block parties, treasure hunts, games of tag,
and delicious barbecues.
They were all a part of life for these kids.

The lazy days of summer,
spent in an inflatable pool,
the smell of suntan lotion is so strong,
its scent lingered on with you,
even after a spectacular sunset.

Early mornings spent on the porch,
eating glazed donuts with cold milk.
Yes, the lazy days of summer
were spent well by the children.

But soon that time faded,
she and her family moved away.
Best friends torn apart,
by miles of endless road.

Buzzing chain saws took the place
of kid's voices.
Childhood houses were knocked down
and larger models set up in their places.

Seven-year-olds became teenagers,
who outgrew their strollers, wading pools,
and scooters.
The powerful thump of speakers,
was heard pouring out of second-story windows.

Though many houses may be gone,
and kids off to college and fancy prep schools.
the calm, lazy summer memories live on,
in the cold silent street of Arthur.

Rebecca Nevers

Hinsdale Middle School
Hinsdale, IL
Nominated by eighth grade teacher Marilyn Cushing

Graduation Memories

After we have said our last good-byes,
And gone our own separate ways,
We will remember the things
That we have done together,
And in our hearts, those memories will stay.

We will remember the days
That we have played together,
We will remember the friends that we had,
We will remember the times that were happy,
And treasure the times that were sad.

We will hold close the times that were joyous,
We will let go the times of fear,
We will live in the dreams of the future,
We will live in the memories that are dear.

We have grown with our class as a family,
A family rooted in love and care,
We have helped one another through tragic times,
But the happy memories are ones we will share.

We have grown up living in our faith,
We have sung the song of peace,
We have learned to share,
What our hearts can give,
And to love, greatest and our least.

And yet times have been hard upon the way,
But we have learned to deal with fate,
We have come to accomplish the impossible,
We have surpassed any obstacles of hate.

But the time has come for us to move on,
God has called us all to be,
Today we will depart from our friends and teachers,
We will move away from our home and family.

God has given us these special times,
To realize how special it's been,
We have learned what it is like to be a family,
A family that will never part to an end.

So as we have said our final good-byes,
And prepare to go on our way,
We will remember the things
That we have done together,
And forever special, those memories will stay.

Andrew D'Amico

St. Raphael
Naperville, IL
Nominated by eighth grade teacher Charlene Paprockas

Japanese Cage Ride

Sway low
silent horse.
Suspended
by a voice
from above.
Galloping away,
bound for
Heaven or Hell.
Whichever one
flings you
away from
your heart
and place
known as home.
It keeps chugging on,
while they
keep wondering
where we went
hiding.
Though I will
always be
enclosed,
set me free.

I know
why they broke
the bonds.
I just wanted
a chance
to say
good-bye.

Lindsey Luebchow

Hinsdale Middle School
Hinsdale, IL
Nominated by eighth grade teacher Marilyn Cushing

On The Inside

I have something on the inside
No one else can see.
I would attempt to show it,
But you wouldn't recognize me.

I'm afraid to tell the truth,
For fear of what you'd say,
I just swallow down my pride,
I'll speak up another day.

I don't want to live more lies,
But I've gotten in so deep,
I don't think the truth will help,
So the secret will have to keep.

Would you judge me, would you hate me
If I told what I was about?
Would you turn your back or leave my side
If I let the real me out?

Maybe you could understand
If I let the truth preside,
But I know we both have something else
Hidden......on the inside.

Lena Hann

Somonauk Jr. High
Somonauk, IL
Nominated by eighth grade teacher Pam Miller

Rain

Rain is like my favorite song,
It reminds me of the melody.
Rain has a beat.
Sometimes hard and fast, sometimes soft and slow.
Rain is like a scary story, dark and wet and terrifying.
Rain is a praise of Light.
Rain is a praise of Darkness.
Rain is a sign of Life.
Rain is a sign of Death.
Rain is an act of an Angel.
Rain is an act of a Demon.
Rain is congruent to Joy and Peace.
Rain is congruent to Pain and Sorrow.
Rain is confusing.
Rain drifts me off to sleep.
Rain wakes me up at night.
When it rains, I love to listen to it.

It comforts me and at the same time, it horrifies me.
Rain has a smell that is wet and clean.
Rain has a smell that is damp and dirty.
Rain brings out all the jolly,
Little worms crawling out of the wet soil
To rejoice over the miracle of rain.

Charlotte Barnes

Oak Elementary
Hinsdale, IL
Nominated by eighth grade teacher T. Bloom

Hate

Hate,
Is a strong word,
So why do we use it?
Sometimes at friends for telling forbidden secrets.
Or at parents for early curfews,
and denying you the right to go out with friends.
But, do we really mean it?
Do we just use it when everything in our naive world
has lost all meaning?
When everything has built up,
until all you want to do is run.
To get away from everything,
That's made you cry.
That has hurt you or that,
made you feel distraught or alone.
You run not knowing where to go or who to talk to,
It makes you think you,
have no one to turn to,
no one to comfort you.
Or to stand by you,
in your time of need.
You wish you were a
bird so you can fly away.
To get away from the,
awfulness that surrounds you.

You cry so hard you feel,
as if you are choking.
You stand there alone in your
flood of tears and hole of suffrage.
You wish someone would love you
with all the love in the world,
to cover you like a warm blanket.
You realize it's only a word.
But it's still powerful
and has gigantic force over the human mind.
Hate can kill.
You must be careful how you use it.
You could drive someone to the edge.
Hate,
Is a strong word.
So why do we use it?

Melissa Morgan

Gregory Middle School
Naperville, IL
Nominated by eighth grade teacher Lynne Ludwig

The Colors Of Fall

As the sun hovers above the spectrum of colors
in the dawn sky, the dew on the hills glistens
as if a silver blanket were thrown over.
As the first rays of light shine through the trees,
like the gold heart of a champion,
the wind sounds like the laughter of a tree nymph.
Crisp leaves flutter like butterflies into the autumn sky.

Aleena Sheikh

Gregory Middle School
Naperville, IL
Nominated by eighth grade teacher Lynne Ludwig

Footprints In The Snow

When I run through the snow
I make footprints
Sometimes I find them again
then it's weird
Think about how and why it was made
then suddenly like a jack-in-the-box,
realize, life is short
Cannot waste one moment
do what you have ever wanted, desired

Hear the snow crunch, crush
breathe in the swirls of brisk air
See an ocean of white stars in an urban jungle
smell the brash wood burn
Feel perspiration creeping down the backside
the mind says, "pick it up, pick it up"
Then leg raises, heart bursts
thrust down and leave a print in the snow

Brian A. Waite

Gregory Middle School
Naperville, IL
Nominated by eighth grade teacher Lynne Ludwig

Unwritten

My mind is like an unwritten novel.
Sometimes it is full of empty pages
just waiting to be filled with
thoughts
and
ideas,
feelings
and
emotions.
Other times it is like an infinite world of
wisdom
and
knowledge.
The stories it holds can be
funny or sad,
romantic or tragic.
It can reflect upon memories
and
bring one back to the past
or
away into the future.
My mind is like an unwritten novel...

Kate Sigel

Madison Jr. High School
Naperville, IL
Nominated by eighth grade teacher Patricia Franzen

Tornado

Howling winds.
Deafening roar.
Mass devastation.
Tornado.

When it comes
You will know.
Rumbling like a train.
But it isn't.
A huge maelstrom of destruction.
Total annihilation.
Tornado.

Car overturner.
Home smasher.
Life stealer.
Fear this whirlwind of death.
Tornado.

Brian Bertram

Madison Jr. High School
Naperville, IL
Nominated by eighth grade teacher Patricia Franzen

Unicorn

The clouds are cut with gold feathered wings.
Its wild mane whips its bare back
With a lasting feeling that stings.

It glides through the air with magic and grace.
Its suede-soft skin is as fair as white lace.

Its nostrils flare inhaling fresh night perfumes.
Its floating shadow explores the vast lands
Of silence as in a deadly tomb.

Its features are piercing as it slices clouds of cotton.
Though by the waking of morning all is forgotten.

The ghostly-white figure is foggy,
Washed away from days of dreams,
Though as the moon glows in the dusted night sky,
The unicorn of mysteries tangos with star beams.

Katie Ryan

Madison Jr. High School
Naperville, IL
Nominated by eighth grade teacher Patricia Franzen

Ancestors

Wrapped in the cloth of the earth
And brought to others in vain
Our ancestors give us birth.

Confined to the chains of misery
Denied the right to be really free
Our ancestors bring us hope.

Dealt a hand in the game of racism
Broken spirits from the words of criticism
Our ancestors give us truth.

Never letting them put us down
Gee! Look what we've accomplished now
Our ancestors give us dreams for the future.

Amina Joyce Egwiekhor

St. James School
Chicago, IL
Nominated by eighth grade teacher Katherine Hlavach

On My Own

Look into my eyes
And tell me what you see
You can see all the pain I've held inside
With any doubt of belief

I've tried so hard
To make people understand
That through the rest of my life
I do not need a helping hand

I know now
I can stand on my own two feet
And go through the rest of my days
Without anyone supporting me

I am a strong, young woman
Who's been through many hard times
I need love and respect
Which took awhile to find

So if you haven't got the message by now
It may take awhile
So you'd better sit down

If you feel as if you're about to fall off your feet
Read this poem a few more times
Until you know that you and your family
Are the only people you need

Nina Soto

Oscar Mayer
Chicago, IL
Nominated by eighth grade teacher Sylvia White

Deepest Thoughts

My dearest Father,
I have You in my mind,
I have You in my heart,
I have You in my soul.
Wherever I go You appear.
I don't know if it's an illusion,
or if it's a dream.
One thing I know for certain
is that You are really here.
I could easily feel Your presence,
You fill the room with Your warmth, love,
and Holy Spirit.
You are with me in the good times,
and in the bad You carry me right through.
You are in every corner of this very room,
watching over all Your children.
Regardless of what people might say about You,
I know You are very true.
In my mind, in my heart and in my soul,
You always make me glow.
Every time I can,
I thank You for the living,
and pray for the dead.
You are the one and only,
I will never forget.

You gave me life,
You gave me breath,
You gave me knowledge,
and You will give me death.
You are true,
You are deep,
You are pure,
You are irreplaceable.
There is not enough time in the world,
to express how grateful I am,
that You gave me life, health, and happiness.
I dedicate this poem to You,
with all my heart and soul.
Thank You for everything You have given me,
my dearest Father, God.

Jacqueline Huerta

Oscar Mayer
Chicago, IL
Nominated by eighth grade teacher Sylvia White

Sunny Days

Sunny days are slow in coming.
Sunny days are when birds are humming.

Sunny days aren't messing with drugs.
Sunny days are getting kisses and hugs.

Sunny days are when you wear shorts and pants.
Sunny days are when you hear songs
that put you in a trance.

Sunny days are when flowers bloom.
Sunny days are when you can go swimming.
Sunny days are when you play with your pet Lemming.

Sunny days are never a nasty gloom.
Sunny days are a blast that go boom, boom, boom!

Sunny days are water trickling down a stream.
Could it be, sunny days are nothing but a dream?

Andrew Z. Stevenson

George W. Curtis Elementary
Chicago, IL
Nominated by eighth grade teacher Cellina Pettiford

Sister

Tears of sadness
She's gone away
On a gloomy winter's day
In death she was taken from me
As the car hit the tree
The boy she had loved so dear
Had caused her the greatest fear
He said for her he would care
So in him she placed her trust
And letting him drive she thought she must
She screamed so loud, they were going so fast
But all of this is in the past
They hit the tree with a sickening thud
Out of my face drained my blood
My dear sister is dead, she is gone for good
Happening to her, it never should
She was innocent and did nothing wrong
Now it is for her that I long
My sister has been taken away
A price she didn't deserve to pay
But the greatest tragedy ever thunk
Might just happen if you're driving drunk

Amanda McCullough

St. Mary Star of the Sea School
Chicago, IL
Nominated by eighth grade teacher Mariza Cascone

Life Road

Life has many paths and turns.
One day, you might be deluged with bliss.
The next you could be filled with revulsion
and sorrow.
You might feel like a splendiferous person today,
but a macabre one tomorrow.
You might be overwhelmed with praise one day.
You might be derided as an imbecile the next.
You might choose to get through life
by telling pretexts.
You might choose to be amoral.
You might choose to be uncouth and obstreperous.
You might choose to follow your dream or vocation.
You might follow your parents' adjuration.
You will be faced with ordeals in your life.
You will be faced with hardships and rigor.
You will be faced with tragedies and adversities.
You will be flush with dolor and a lack of vigor.

These are the obstacles of life
which we must learn to sustain.
We will have many difficult experiences and pain.
The choices we make in life are the paths
we choose to take.

We're bound to take turns that are mistakes,
and when we do, we must learn to remain stalwart
and get back on track.
The decisions we make are ours and ours alone.
Our life is the most precious thing we own.
We learn to live and we live to learn.
We travel the road and take many turns.
We push ourselves to prosper in life
and are stimulated by goads,
as we travel this long labyrinthine life road.

Ryan Leung

St. Mary Star of the Sea School
Chicago, IL
Nominated by eighth grade teacher Mariza Cascone

The perfect family exists in me,
It is a vision of what I hope it will be.
There is only one thing that matters to me,
It's the people I love; it's my family.

I could not picture my family without me,
Without me it would be an atrocity.
But the perfect family is what I hoped it would be.
Because the perfect family will always include me!

Dedicated to my perfect family -- The Panjwani's
and to Mrs. Maude Turner, thank you!

Ali Panjwani

Richard Edward
Chicago, IL
Nominated by eighth grade teacher Maude Turner

Someone No One Knew

There once was a perfect child,
She always was the best,
No one liked her,
But did anyone know her?
She was so confused,
She felt all alone,
She hated what she was.
Put on a show no longer,
Be perfect no more,
She will live like the rest,
But she is like the rest,
She doesn't know.
Run,
Find your path,
Seek guidance, child.
She needs help,
No, she needs strength,
She can do anything.
Stop the act,
Be yourself,
People will like you.

Jenny Baker

St. Florian
Chicago, IL
Nominated by eighth grade teacher Lynn Mitchell

The Definition Of Love

Love is gentle, love is kind
In some cases true love can be hard to find
Love is loving, loving is sweet
Love is simple, like tickling your loved one's feet
Love is strange, but it can be funny
Love is calm, like a spring day that's sunny
Love is easy, love is hard
Love can be tear-jerking, like giving somebody
a meaningful Valentine's Day card
Love is courteous, it isn't mean
Love isn't quick-tempered, but instead it's serene
Love is natural, all from the heart
Love is being together,
knowing you two will never part
Love is graceful, it is a treat
Hopefully one day I will meet someone that's sweet
My definition of love
is when the heart and soul mends,
I hate to say it, but this is where my definition ends!

Michelle Ruiz

St. Paul Lutheran
Chicago, IL
Nominated by eighth grade teacher Michael Heinze

Night

So very wild yet extremely tame,
If you listen closely you can hear it call your name.
It is black as unburned coal,
It rages against the day but is calm in its soul.
It leaves with the coming of daylight,
But is guaranteed to come back tonight.

S. Michael Pape

Hanson Park School
Chicago, IL
Nominated by eighth grade teacher Mrs. Sylvana Kohnen

Windows

Your eyes...
A window to your soul
Revealing your deepest secrets
Allowing your hopes and dreams to run free

Your smile...
A window to your heart
Unlocking your emotions
Forever protecting me from the dangers of life

Your heart...
A window to your love
But also to your friendship
For each is a beautiful prize

Yourself...
A beautiful gift
Bringing light to the world
And also to my heart

Julie Gorzkowski

St. Monica
Chicago, IL
Nominated by eighth grade teacher Virginia Whittaker

Under My Couch

As I put my hand under my couch,
I seem to find a little pouch.
My little bird,
How did he get out?
Some sandwich crusts,
A pair of socks,
A telephone cord,
What? This should be on the telephone!
I sink much deeper,
And what do I find?
The ship from Titanic,
A mime from 1909.
I scream as I find a little rat,
A baby hat from when I was two,
A mouse from Mars,
With a huge laser gun,
Wait this is my brother's.
At last I found what I was looking for,
A little teddy bear,
To hang upon my door.

Angela Patsiopoulos

Jamieson Elementary School
Chicago, IL
Nominated by eighth grade teacher
Demetra Antonopoulos

Who Am I?

I was born sixty-two years ago.
To proud parents.
Who am I?

I was a high school dropout many years ago.
I was married to a runaway girl.
Who am I?

I had an hour of fame long ago.
I had my name in lights.
Who am I?

I fell from grace not long ago.
But I heard the beat go on.
Who am I?

I was lost in the desert not long ago.
But I found the way to the hill.
Who am I?

I think I hear
Michael shout: "Look out!"
Who am I?

I served on the hill
And died on the hill.
Who am I?

Michael Russell

Ebinger
Chicago, IL
Nominated by eighth grade teacher Jessica Chethik

Lifeless Eyes

A tragic life-changing moment in time,
the first I realized life was not easy...
My aged adventurous great-uncle's life was exquisite,
until a man of vengeance appeared in his life,
his eyes filled with fire and fear,
his face a mask of evil,
a shaking hand held a gun,
threatened my uncle and his family.
Valiantly my uncle fought for his life.
Seconds later a shot...
and my uncle lay down with lifeless eyes.
Two died that night, yet one still lives.
The butchery occurred
in front of my aunt's living eyes.
Now catatonic eyes that remain open,
but do not see.
Nothing remains but a weak voice repeating,
"I could have helped but I did not."

Millions of minutes have passed since that night.
Thousands of memories of what was,
but can never be again,
flash through my mind.
And I know the fear in my heart will never truly
leave...

Farah Merchant

Stone Academy
Chicago, IL
Nominated by eighth grade teacher Ms. Hellmann

The Ship Of Dreams

"The Ship of Dreams" was what it was called,
By some but not by all.
To some it was a "Death Trap,"
Taking them home -- that's all.

To others it was splendid;
"A ship with everything!"
A home with cars, rooms,
And practically anything.

It went out to sea,
For its first time and last.
And then hit an iceberg,
Sank, and landed in our past.

It was in 1912
When the ship hit ocean floors,
And there it'd forever stay,
With all the broken doors.

We can't change history,
Which everyone will know;
And as long as we live
This history will always grow.

We cannot change history,
Or experience how it feels;
Because it already happened,
The ship's under our heels.

For Titanic was a ship,
Of everyone's dreams;
"A millionaire's home,"
That's what it seems...

Not only millionaires,
But poor went too;
And sank to the ocean floors,
As everything would do.

Titanic, Titanic
If it wouldn't have sank
I'd have one person --
And that's God to thank.

Dorothy Bobak

Richard Edward
Chicago, IL
Nominated by eighth grade teacher Maude Turner

Utterly Confused

I'm over you, I'm not
If only I knew
I often wonder if you still care
My mind debates
If you cared
You'd still be here

What is it I hold onto
Memories
Or is it you
Sweet memories I still have
Sweet memories that make me so sad

Why is it I feel alone
In the past all I wanted
Was for you to go
Here I am
Left so lonely
Here I am
Thinking of you

My thoughts run deep
The more I weep
There's sadness with each thought

Each time a thought is opened
I feel the pain
Pulling me apart

I need someone
To guide me away
From dreadful days
If no one comes
I will force myself up
And leave

Why must I be so
Utterly confused
Why can't I look at my problem
And know what to do
I'm not the only one
I'm not alone
But I'm the only one with my problem
The saddest I've ever known

Cherise Lopez

Columbus Elementary School
Cicero, IL
Nominated by eighth grade teacher Nancy Lunon

Don't Hide Behind The Mask

Why hide behind the mask,
And cover your unique, beautiful
Black face.
Hold your head up high,
And show your pride.
Don't settle for less,
Always do your best.
Self-esteem,
Is my theme.

We as people,
We all have our ups and
Downs;
But don't wear a frown.

Don't let people hold you
Back, because they don't want
To achieve in life;
And that's a fact!!!

Why do I say, "Don't hide
Behind the mask,"
It's to persuade you to

Have an open mind.
Don't swallow your pride,
And speak your mind.

Say it loud and clear,
So everyone can hear
I am a leader, not a follower,
I have pride, I'm an achiever.
I have respect for myself,
And others.

And I have confidence.
So come from behind that mask,
And show what you have to
Offer.
Don't hide behind the Mask!

Class of 1998

Kietta McFee

Higgins Community Academy
Chicago, IL
Nominated by eighth grade teacher E. Johnson

My First Love

You have a great smile
That no one can resist
You walk by me
I almost melt like a chocolate in the heat
Every time I try to talk to you
I feel butterflies tickling my stomach
I laugh instead and you laugh back at me
I say to myself
This is a weird sensation that
I have never felt before
I discover that it is
The great feeling of my first love
Since then every time I go to bed
I think and I pray about you and
I know there is no one like you.

Diana Fernandez

Our Lady of the Mount
Cicero, IL
Nominated by eighth grade teacher Bernadette Kec

Wondering What

I sit and I reminisce where my father's at
What he's wearing
How he looks
I love him in my heart
even though I don't know him
I have a deep anger inside
that I hate him for leaving me
I'll never know the reason
he walked out of my life so suddenly
or if he's ever gonna walk right back in it
he's like a storm
you never know when they're going to appear
and when they're going to disappear
I was hoping this storm would stay
awhile longer

Lindsay Platz

PBL Jr. High
Paxton, IL
Nominated by eighth grade teacher Arcelia Watson

Friends

People come to me with their problems
but I cannot help.
They think I'm perfect
but I'm not.
I listen and listen
but I cannot talk.
I am shocked at what I hear.
They have problems
so do I.
I listen some more
but I can't anymore.
I stop them...
we hug, we cry...
We know what is wrong
we know it's not us,
it's our lives.
I have pretended...
but I can't anymore.
You are not perfect
nor am I.
We must go hand in hand
with our problems.
We must face the world
with its problems.

We must help each other
and not fight.
There must be peace
between all humankind.
We must be friends until the end of time.

Dedicated to all my friends whom I always will adore.

Jenny Ruth Jones Dale

Inter-American Magnet
Chicago, IL
Nominated by eighth grade teacher Lilia Calvimontes

Shadow That I Am

I am the shadow that follows.
I am always listening, always vigilant.
I am last, but almost never first.
If I am first they just shrug me off as to the cold.
My heart cries out, but no one is there to listen.
Because I am a shadow, invisible, yet still there.

I have a friend, but that might not be the correct term.
I follow and I listen like the shadow that I am.
I try to answer questions, but I am cut off too soon.
I help when it is asked of me,
I give advice when they need it,
But that is almost the only time
they see me standing in the dark.
When I need the same
they are scattered like the leaves in the wind.
They have left me drowning in a sea of helplessness.
They say that we are friends,
but what is the definition of a friend?
A person who is there to help,
there to care for and support you.
I am, but they are not.

Another time I am noticed
is when I do something stupid
or say something foolish.
That is when I become a person,
to be beaten down and ridiculed.
I try to rise back up, but I feel like I am falling.
Forever falling, never to rise again.
Please, oh please someone catch me!
But they cannot catch me because I am a shadow.
I am.like the sand, I will slip through their fingers.
Yes, they will catch some of me,
just enough to see the pain in my life.
For I am a shadow always vigilant, always listening.

Rachel M. Ens

PBL Jr. High
Paxton, IL
Nominated by eighth grade teacher Arcelia Watson

Looking Past

Living with a disability
is hard and nowhere near easy
It may be hard to do everyday things
It may even be hard to answer the phone when it rings

He may have trouble walking
His speech may be slurred or slow
but if you can look past these frailties
you, yourself, will discover you'll grow

We've all been granted special gifts
which makes us each unique
It could be as simple as a smile
or happiness we bring

Riches can be measured in many ways,
in what things you have or gain
But it can also be measured by what you give up
when helping those in need

It's easy to avoid or ignore
those different than you and me
The hardest part is recognizing
that in God's eyes He sees us equally

Heroes are not just athletes
measured in strength and speed
They're children without such gifts
who struggled to walk, and read

If we used the same energy
we use to criticize
to help those less fortunate
we'd help them to rise

Did you ever wonder
what we could be seeing
if we looked past the surface
to the greatness in each being?

John A. Halerz II

Queen of Martyrs
Chicago, IL
Nominated by eighth grade teacher Lois Kettering

The Unfortunate Traveler

A man travels around the world
To give poems to different lands
So he went to a country to unfurl
His many papers held with rubber bands.

On his way to Istanbul
He came upon an ugly man,
Who asked him for a bit of gruel.
And the traveler said he can.

But the ugly man was not a man
Not a man of handsome wits,
He cut the gruel in many slits,
And said, "I want a sunny tan."

The traveling man thought this queer,
So he cleaned his right and left ear.
In his mind he knew it wrong,
To hit the man with a two-ton thong.

Later in the traveler's life,
He came upon his future wife
He did not know this in the least.
Because he put her on a leash.

This conduct made her very mad
It also made the traveler sad,
To think of such a precious prize.
Should be very meanly pulled down to size.

When the time was right for the traveler to die,
He knew it right to say good-bye.
He gave his papers to his sons,
Who thought them as funny puns.

Troy Axis Kunath

Capron Elementary
Capron, IL
Nominated by eighth grade teacher Toni Dietrich

Hold On To Your Dreams

Hold on to your dreams,
and don't let go,
They're more important,
than one can know.

Dreams are the future,
without them are fears,
Mankind will be left,
with only its tears.

Men sailed the waters,
others soared through the sky,
Who'd ever imagine,
a machine that could fly.

Cities built in the deserts,
in hot blazing sand,
Telephones connecting us with,
people in far distant lands.

A mouse and his kingdom,
which brings joy to our hearts,
All were mere dreams,
all had their starts.

So hold on to your dreams,
without them is sorrow,
But with them comes hope,
for a better tomorrow.

Valerie Casey

St. Monica
Chicago, IL
Nominated by eighth grade teacher Virginia Whittaker

What Is This World Coming To

The world is full of violence and drugs
what is going to change it.
We need people that will stand up for the world
and in everyone's rights.
Who will take a stand
and help all the homeless people with nowhere to go.
They need a place to call home.
They all need food in their stomachs
and a roof over their heads
to keep them from the cold and rough world.
One day I will be one of those people
that will save the world,
and help the homeless find a home.

Brandy R. Morris

Capron Elementary
Capron, IL
Nominated by eighth grade teacher Toni Dietrich

The Joust

In his hand he held his shield.
He knew with his charge he should not yield.
With lance in hand, his steed snorted steam,
He knew this would not be like a dream.
If he lost here and now he wouldn't wake,
His life would be the knight's to take.
The queen sat with the king who is just,
The knight did not know who to trust.
The squire shouted in clear voice, "Charge!"
The knight on the other side looked enormously large.
He held out his shield and lance,
While the jester in the courtyard happily pranced.
In a matter of seconds the knight lay on the ground,
All of the people near him did surround.
Then the knight knew he should have stayed in bed,
And now he lies on the ground cold and dead.

Kyle Swartz

St. Anne School
Dixon, IL
Nominated by eighth grade teacher Sarah Stonesifer

Life Is Precious

Something's wrong with me,
I don't know the answer
I need therapy

I'm in deep thought,
complete concentration
I feel as though I'm falling
through a deep, dark hole

With what I know, my life
is nothing, worth no value,
I am nothing...then, I realize
I am someone and I have
something to strive for, something
to stay alive for

I am loved, people care for me;
they embrace me
I matter -- a revelation, realization
my life is worth living

Everyone's life is good, now
I know my life should,
be lived to the fullest

Now I know all people
are special and unique, everyone
has been made complete --
Life is precious and should
never be taken for granted

I can't believe I just thought about that horrible,
most terrible thing,
that could've cut me off like an unwanted string,
something that could've changed my life forever

Monica Hermes

St. Mary's School
Dixon, IL
Nominated by eighth grade teacher Amy Godbold

I Want To Be...

I love animals.
Animals are great.
I am pretty sure animals are part of my fate.
I want to be a veterinarian.

I love people.
People are kind
People you can always find.
Some people need lots of help.
I want to be a physical therapist.

I love outdoors.
Outside is lovely.
I like to predict the weather.
I want to be a meteorologist.

I love volcanoes.
Volcanoes are an awesome force of nature.

I would like to study them.
I want to be a volcanologist.

But right now
I want to be....

An eighth grader!!!!

Sarah Frogge

Maternity B.U.M.
Bourbonnais, IL
Nominated by eighth grade teacher Mrs. Horstmann

I Am

I am someone's best friend.
I am a person that is kind.
I could have cured cancer.
I could have saved someone's life.
I am an inspiration.
I am a poet.
I am me,
but for when I am me,
I am destroyed.
My mother doesn't want me,
my father hates me.
I am a blob to them.
I am just a thing to them.
For I am still their child,
but they still destroy me.
I may be vulnerable,
but I am God's creation.
And when one destroys me,
they are destroying my God.

Darcy Dunphy

St. Mary's School
Dixon, IL
Nominated by eighth grade teacher Amy Godbold

She dances in,
in green and clad in jewel-like blooms
rosy and glowing.

Uplifting serenity,
a bringing of life to
shadowed corners.

She waltzes through the spaces
and smiles,
leaving warmth with those she touches.

They are awakening, yawning and stretching
their arms to the sky,
greeted with new garments.

Casting off the old darkness
and cold,
friendly and conversational again.

Summer greets the earth,
and all is alive.

Carolyn Beth Albert

Freeport Junior High
Freeport, IL
Nominated by eighth grade teacher Michele Elzen

Grandpa

You were a person,
Very close to me.
You were my grandpa.

I always thought that when
I came to see you,
You would be waiting.

I took your presence for granted,
And when you went away,
I realized what I had lost.

I remember everything,
How when I would come to see you,
You would smile at me.
How we talked to each other,
Without using words.
You would call to Grandma,
To get you a drink,
When you could have got it yourself,
And then you would smile at me,
And I knew you were being funny.

I was always worried about you.
You only had one lung,
And breathing was hard for you to do.
But you always said you were fine.

I didn't spend as much time with you,
As I could have,
And now that makes me sad.
But you always were winking at me,
And I knew that you loved me.

When you went into the hospital,
Your room was so dull,
So I brought you a beautiful poster,
Of a horse running,
And hung it up on the wall.
You told me it was just what you needed,
That you would think,
Of me every time you looked at it.

Then when you went into the rehabilitation center,
I gave up going out to eat,
To stay with you.
I knew that was the best thing,
I could do for you.

My mom says I had a special
Connection with you.
And I think I did.

Now, the St. Rita painting is in memory of you,
And no one will know what exactly,
Your life was like,
But you will live in the painting.

I miss you so much,
But I know you are not suffering.
I never understood what I had,
Until I lost it.

But you will always be with me,
In my life and in my heart.
I love you, Grandpa,
And I know that you love me too.

Jennifer Wilbur

Maternity B.U.M.
Bourbonnais, IL
Nominated by eighth grade teacher Mrs. Horstmann

Emotions

Emotions are like a key,
a key that opens a door
to a person's whole life.
When you mess with
a person's emotions, it
is like you are messing
with fire.
Be careful or you will get
burned.
When you mess with
someone's emotions that
person becomes very upset.
So upset that they might
do something that they
will regret. So I advise
you not to mess with
someone's emotions because
when you mess with
someone's emotions that person
will get hurt.
Emotions hurt; believe me.

Kelley Marie Otten

Jordan Catholic School
Rock Island, IL
Nominated by eighth grade teacher Catherine Plasschaert

Don't Be Afraid

Woke up this morning, felt a little down.
In a little while I'm going to start school,
a world I have never been around.

I said out loud, "I don't want to go to a new school,"
when all of a sudden Elmo said, "I think you do."

Let my friends and I tell you everything you would do
at this new school.

Mr. Count came out and said,
"They're going to teach you how to count
one through one hundred."

Cookie Monster interrupted, "Don't you worry.
You're going to be eating snacks every day
only if you behave."

Bert and Ernie walked out and pronounced,
"There is a time in the day where you can sing
and play and use your imagination to build
a world of fascinating creation."

"I don't know. I'm still unsure.
I heard that school is a big place
with big kids as tall as mountains.
I think they will run over me."

Out of nowhere marched Big Bird who stated,
"Little friend, don't you be afraid.
Gonzo will come and save the day.
Hey, if Gonzo isn't around, ask a teacher.
They're never far away."

"Elmo knows you will enjoy school,
everyone from Sesame Street told you so.
Just remember you're never alone."

"I'm ready to go to school.
I just wish I could begin right now."

Katherine Linden

Jordan Catholic School
Rock Island, IL
Nominated by eighth grade teacher Catherine Plasschaert

The River

I am a river, proud and true
Strong as a lion, yet meek as a lamb
I can be loud as thunder, but quiet as a dove's coo

I am a river, powerful and brave
Venturing where only the most brave dare
Off to explore the sea and any cave

I am a river, fierce and wild
My rapids rock and turn nearly every boat
The horror story of a child

I am a river, steady in my flow
Only to turn to view a mountain crown
I may end as the ocean's feast, but that I do not know

I am a river, gentle and kind
Barely strong enough to rock a baby's bed
Yet I am only thought so in a certain mind

I am a river, sensitive and tender
As clear as a maiden's veil
Or dark as a midnight splendor

I am a river, proud and true

Elicia Grace

Stephen Mack Middle School
Rockton, IL
Nominated by eighth grade teacher Cynthia Moberg

The Puddle

The wind,
Sharp and cold.
Whisked pathways in

The leaves
Ever
Falling
From
The foliage.

One,
A lonely oak,
Last of its generation,
Drifted into

A puddle,
Clean and clear,
Also last of its generation.

Together
They await the

Son,
Bright and warming,
With the rest of us.

Amber Andress

Rockridge Junior High
Taylor Ridge, IL
Nominated by eighth grade teacher Kathleen C. Eppel

Snow In January

Trudging through the snow in January,
Is my least favorite thing.
There is no reason for the birds to sing.
The snow pounds hard,
And sends chills through my heart.
All the flurries, no matter how soft,
I know that no one will call school off.
"This is a pain!" I say aloud,
And up the street comes a big yellow plow.
I know that the bus will follow,
I know that it will.
So that I may go to school
And let my knowledge spill.

Drew DeSmet

Rockridge Junior High
Taylor Ridge, IL
Nominated by eighth grade teacher Kathleen C. Eppel

If You Just Try

You can be anything if you try,
So don't give up and let yourself die.
Get an education, that's a start,
Go to school and make yourself smart.
Set your own goals and work it all the way,
You can do it, day-by-day.
You can ask for help whenever you need,
Work your own pace, work your own speed.
Give it a try and make yourself proud,
Don't get lost in the wrong crowd.
If you get lost and don't know what to do,
There will always be someone there for you.
Give it an effort and then you'll see,
You can be anything you want to be.
Always remember one thing more,
Never give up or you won't score.

Erika Ward

Potnam County Jr. High
McNabb, IL
Nominated by eighth grade teacher Nancy Hopkins

What Am I To Do?

What are you to do?
When your supposed friend doesn't seem to like you.

Why did she change so fast?
Why doesn't our friendship ever seem to last?

I wonder if she ever really liked me in the first place.
I wonder if she ever had to force a smile upon her face.

She seems so cold now, so stubborn and dry.
I know I should sometime,
but it's just too hard to ask her why.

She never returns my phone calls,
now isn't that strange.
How the phone once rung off the hook,
but now everything's changed.

She used to tell me all the time,
"You're my best friend."

Now I realize how fast some things
can come to an end.

I must ask her now to see if this is all true.
But when I ask, and if it is; what am I to do?

Shelley Elizabeth Backos

Rutland Community District #230
Ottawa, IL
Nominated by eighth grade teacher Pamela Stack

Tomorrow

Tomorrow everything will be all right,
and everybody will be fine.
But sooner or later, I'll find out,
that's only in my mind.

Tomorrow I will go everywhere,
and I'll be free to fly.
But those things will never come
unless I really try.

Tomorrow I will be happy,
without a speck of worry.
I can only hope that
Tomorrow would really hurry.

Tomorrow everything will be perfect,
without one mistake.

But my only conclusion is
that Tomorrow must be fake.

Tomorrow is the beginning of my life,
and that's all I have to say.
But just let me make one thing clear,
Tomorrow won't come today.

Julie Elizabeth Aubry

Rutland Community District #230
Ottawa, IL
Nominated by eighth grade teacher Pamela Stack

Memories

Senseless emotions swept away
Memories of the past remembered today
We laughed so hard we almost cried
Our hearts said hello when our minds said good-bye
The wind echoes your scent that was left behind
Looking for today, tomorrow we will find
Tear-streaked eyes that never cried
Speechless mouths that always asked why
Dreams that came from sleepless nights
Whatever was wrong always seemed right

Imaginary feelings suddenly became real
Hearts we could touch but never feel
Vines wrapped around a helpless heart
Unknown sorrows that were there from the start
Suddenly searching for a speck of light
Instead found a darkness incredibly bright
Filling in space as it empties out
Laughter and cries danced about
Bringing a life to the darkness of death
To some love is unknown, but clear to the rest

Kate Hasler

Von Steuben Middle
Peoria, IL
Nominated by eighth grade teacher Arnitria Shaw

Clouds

Clouds are like eagles soaring about the world,
gliding on the wind currents as their only motion while
watching the ground from their distant position.
They care not of where they're going
and even less where they came from.
From dawn until dusk they float aimlessly
among a sea of blue
only to make faces in our imaginations;
rolling across the sky as if giant cotton balls
or flowing together to make a sea of their own.
They wave to-and-fro in a balancing act
until a small stumble reveals a small ray of sunshine
slipping through.

Nikki Ferre

Washington Gifted School
Peoria, IL
Nominated by eighth grade teacher A. J. Schroff

In A World

In a world of confusion
I've been found.
Found by the One who loves me
And keeps me safe from harm.
Found so that I can find others
When they are lost.

In a world of sin
I've been forgiven.
Forgiven for my many faults
Committed throughout my life
Forgiven for my failures
By the light of my life.

In a world of many
I've been chosen.
Chosen to lead a path for others
To make their way by.
Chosen to believe in the unbelievable
And expect the unexpected.

In a world of hate
I've been loved.
Loved with the warmest touch
That could ever be experienced.

Loved so much that I learn to love others
With His hand holding mine
And guiding me
When I find,
When I fail,
When I lead, and
When I love.

In a world of despair
I've been blessed.

Sarah Nelson

Washington Gifted School
Peoria, IL
Nominated by eighth grade teacher A. J. Schroff

97

One Answer

So many questions,
But answers?
I suppose there were once,
But now, long forgotten.
Forgotten among the trails of life.
But if life is nothing but looking for answers
That your questions disguise,
What is it?
And if you are looking for answers you will never find,
How can there be peace?
Can peace only be found in death,
When there is no life?
But if there is no life,
What good is it to have peace?
This is why some of the greater questions
Are not asked.
But the answer is there.
Maybe it is because they do not want to find it.
Probably not though,
Because who wouldn't want better?
So, the people live their ordinary lives,
Never knowing, dreaming, imagining
That there is something extraordinary waiting.
And only those who reach toward the extraordinary

Find peace in life,
And life in death.
As for the rest, they think they know the answer.
But one day, when faced with the question,
They will find their answer has failed them.
And then where will they be?
They may spend their lives
Searching for an answer to cling to,
Never reaching into the darkness,
Lighting a candle,
And illuminating what was always there.
But perhaps they will join the dreamers,
Who know the one true answer.
The secret that everyone can find
If they want to.
And if everyone can know,
Is it really a secret?
So many questions,
But only one answer.

D'Arcy Rapp

Washington Gifted School
Peoria, IL
Nominated by eighth grade teacher A. J. Schroff

Satin Saloon

The feather plume
Rises from her head
Like birds waving in the
Wind.
She walks down the dusty
Road as
Tumbleweeds roll by.

She lifts her skirts,
Red satin once soft now
Parched like her throat.
Black lace glove
Brushes her golden
Hair from her damp
Forehead.
She enters a saloon
Filled with
Primitive men drinking
Hard liquor.

Passing a table of men
Playing poker, she
Laughs as a man silently
Pulls a spare
Ace from his

Snakeskin boots.
She hopes he doesn't get
Caught.

Sighing, she sits down on a
Stool, orders a whiskey, double, and
Rests her aching feet.
She lets the bitter drink
Glide down her
Throat,
Thankful for the
Icy relief in the
Desert heat.

Nicole Renee Sushka

Tri-Valley Middle School
Downs, IL
Nominated by eighth grade teacher Kristin Prosser

For You

A day goes by and still I cry
For the person I miss, gone away my bliss.
Life no longer living, feelings no longer feeling.
A heart no longer beating,
The layers away are peeling.
Pondering the question why, I feel that I should die.
For you not to be alone, nor I to feel the same.
To take a life away, who should feel the blame?
To finally leave this earth has haunted us from birth.
When will the tears go away? I sit and I pray,
Dear God please keep watch, keep watch day-by-day.
You're finally at peace now, all safe and sound.
Is it safer for you to be under the ground?
I know it was hard for someone like you.
If you let it just once,
Your good would show through.
I know you cared more than it seemed,
When I saw you so happy,
Your face brightly gleamed.
The ups and the downs you had to endure,
All of them said you were insecure,
But I know the truth, I truly do.
They only needed to let you be you!
Now you're all gone and I hope they feel bad.
You were mistreated and you should be mad.

Not one breath left, nor one lone heartbeat.
I'll dig a grave and dig it deep,
Place a statue at your feet.
On the statue I'll place broken chains,
And show the world you're free from your pains.

Karin Winters

Pontiac Junior High
Pontiac, IL
Nominated by eighth grade teacher Mary Passini

This Face In The Mirror

Is this my face I see before me?
This hollow shell which once held a soul?
No, it cannot be, for I loved once.
I loved all you could possibly dream.
The earth, the stars, the Heaven above.
I too loved a man, who blinded me so.
Robbed me of my youth and beauty,
and left me an old withered corpse,
with nothing left, but a broken heart.
Oh mirror, tell me,
am I not the woman I once was?
A woman of strength, courage, spirit?
Or am I just the remains of the woman
who once existed?
Remains, of course,
for I remain the human being
who has faced all of life's trials.
But now, will I become that woman again?

By crossing this path of light and wonder,
will I become the girl I once was?
I was after all, once a woman of courage,
a woman of strength.
Now my strength will live on,
in the great unknown.

Alison Hanold

West Middle School
Alton, IL
Nominated by eighth grade teacher Vickie L. Oberlink

It was a very scary Halloween night
The jack-o'-lantern was flaming with light
The family had left me on my own
Not a soul in the house, just me alone
I was reading a book to occupy my time
THE LEGEND OF SLEEPY HOLLOW,
a favorite of mine
A thought struck me that sounded like joy
I leaped into the air, my plan to employ
I ran from room to room, throughout the house
Scurrying about like a frightened little mouse
I found the treasure for which I did look
The idea would come true, just like in the book
I picked up the pumpkin and thrust it on top
When I smelled something burning I had to stop
I had put the flaming pumpkin on my head
And in the next instant, I fell to the ground, dead
As I looked down on my body
While floating in the sky
I realized the flame had caused my brains to fry

Andrew Galligan

West Middle School
Alton, IL
Nominated by eighth grade teacher Vickie L. Oberlink

Grateful For These Guys

Like a needle in a haystack,
True friends are hard to find.
That's why I am so thankful,
I can call you mine.

Whenever I need a shoulder,
You're there to catch my tears.
You've kept my many secrets,
Through the passing years.

You've been there through my triumphs.
You've witnessed my defeats.
I'll remember the good times,
And pray the bad ones don't repeat.

With you my heart is honest.
There's one thing I've never said.
Thank you for everything you've done.
There's no other friend like you!!

Dedicated to Alisa Creall

Marissa Lynn Wilcut

Southwestern Middle School
Piasa, IL
Nominated by eighth grade teacher Norma Highsmith

The Tornado

Houses torn down, lying on the ground.
Memories blown away, taken by the wind at day.
The hospitals all left filled.
Many people have been killed.
Million of families broken apart.
Nothing left but a broken heart.
Towns falling down 'til there's nothing left but dirt.
Can you feel all of everyone's hurt?
To save anything in their lives it was too late.
Everyone in town was forced to relocate.
Not even knowing what it would cost,
Everything in their lives was now lost.
No one hears a sound,
From the bodies that have not been found.
But tears of pain have now been shed,
For the people that are dead.
One might ask, "What could cause such a disaster?"
The tornado had come much faster.

Tasha Sillivan

Southwestern Middle School
Piasa, IL
Nominated by eighth grade teacher Norma Highsmith

Stay Forever In My Heart

I don't like to say that you went away,
Because in my heart you will always stay.

Stay with me forever young,
Because my life has just begun.

You're in my heart forevermore.
I will never walk out that door.

In my heart I'll be by your side,
Like an angel ready to guide.

Even if I see you no longer,
My love for you could not be stronger.

You're in my heart forevermore.
I will never walk out that door.

Ashliegh Dawn Hull

North Greene Junior High
Roodhouse, IL
Nominated by eighth grade teacher Nancy Rhoades

My Messy Bedroom

I was cleaning my bedroom
and here's what I found:
A history essay that was due in sixth grade
and an old tie-dyed shirt that had begun to fade
A children's ant farm that I had broken
and an out-of-date carnival token
A picture of me with my hair wildly curled
and some Mickey Mouse ears from Disney World
A nasty, disgusting gym sock
and a windup soldier that didn't walk
A jar of molded sticky candy
and a broken record of "Yankee Doodle Dandy"
A supergiant rainbow bouncy ball
and my sister's stupid Barbie doll
A dented trophy from basketball camp
and my father's broken desk lamp
A pair of Nike's that were really stinky
and my messed-up metal Slinky

A useless, rusted house key
and my baby brother's stuffed bumblebee
A pile of toe jam and pocket lint
and a molded stick of peppermint
The last thing I found was my German shepherd, Ruff
and after that, I wondered,
what the heck am I going to do with all this stuff?

Zachary Scott Burrus

North Greene Junior High
Roodhouse, IL
Nominated by eighth grade teacher Nancy Rhoades

Why I Never Smile

Why is my heart so full of sadness
Could it be the life I've been dealt
is so full of madness
Or is it just because I'm always
feeling so blue
Because in my life I have no one
to turn to
Or could it be that I've been dealt
a bad hand
Is this normal for a fifteen-year-old
girl to feel like this
Why do I feel as if there's no one
for me
Or is it just a feeling I can see
For years I've tried to give all
my love
And in the end I end up lonely
and in the dark
To say I'm always happy would
be a lie
Sometimes I feel so sad it's like
I'm going to die

But I hang in there always for
a while
But I'm right back to wondering
I
NEVER
SMILE

Jakeia Bowers

Venice Elementary
Venice, IL
Nominated by eighth grade teacher Ida Buckels

Seasons Of A Slave

The springtime rain.
Falling,
On your hot face.
Falling, falling on your bruised and battered face.
The face that was once proud and beautiful,
Now haggard and worn.

The summer sun.
Beating,
Down on your back.
Beating, beating down on your old and tired back.
While you work all alone in the field,
Expected to work
While the hot sun is beating you down.
The back that was once new and strong and useful,
Now bent and frail.

The autumn leaves.
Changing,
Like you have changed.
Changing, changing, showing bold and brilliant color,
While you wither.
You do not change for the better.
You will not return in body.

The winter snow.
Giving rest to all that is around it,
And all that is under it.
You just wish it would give rest to you.
Or do you?
Can't you see the snow?
It's falling,
Covering you like a blanket.
You feel tired, weak,
And yet you are warm and comforted.
You slowly start to close your eyes,
Slowly,
Slowly,
You fall asleep.

You will not feel
The springtime rain,
Falling.
You will not feel
The hot summer sun,
Beating.
You will not see
The autumn leaves,
Changing.
And you have seen your last
Winter's snow.

Stasia Wylie

St. Albert the Great
Fairview Heights, IL
Nominated by eighth grade teacher Nancy Tanase

Searching For Indigo

If I had to be a color,
I think I would choose Red.
It expresses the warmth I have for others,
and the love that is never dead.

If I had to be a color,
I also could choose Orange,
expressing friendliness and caring --
even in fights that seem like storms.

If I had to be a color,
I'd choose Yellow, the color of the sun.
For it symbolizes the sun bringing
happiness to everyone.

If I had to be a color,
Green could be my choice;
symbolizing the web of the earth
in which everyone has a voice.

If I had to be a color,
I could go with Blue,
symbolizing my sadness, and times
when I do not know what to do.

If I had to be a color,
Violet could be my pick,
symbolizing the depth of my soul
and my heart that is rich.

If I had to be a color,
I would not know which choice to make.
For I am so many things,
I could not choose just one shade.

I would have to be a rainbow
with colors yet unseen;
for there are many sides of me
that no one, not even me, has seen.

Maybe one of them is Indigo.

Katharine Wicklein

Our Lady Queen of Peace School
Belleville, IL
Nominated by eighth grade teacher Rosemary Buss

I Wonder

The wind blows the trees shake,
I wonder what all this will make.
A storm a thunder sound,
I wonder what will be found.
Some rain or maybe some sleet,
I wonder when these two will meet.
I wonder if the sky will fall,
Or maybe nothing will happen at all.

Jaidra Boman

Coulterville Public
Coulterville, IL
Nominated by eighth grade teacher Patti Berry

The Fight

Six o'clock this morning last night,
two dead boys arose a fight.
Back to back they fought each other,
pulled their swords and shot one another.
Two deaf policemen heard the noise,
came to kill the two dead boys.
If you don't believe this lie is true,
ask the blind man he saw it too.

Corey Miller

Coulterville Public
Coulterville, IL
Nominated by eighth grade teacher Patti Berry

A Dance Studio

Mirrors in every corner,
bars on each wall, dust bunnies in the corners,
dirty blue carpet, cups and water bottles on the floor.

The nuances of a dance studio
Smells of sweat, rosin, wet and dry;
cheap bleach on the Poms, Lysol sprayed in the air
to cover up the musty smell.

The nuances of a dance studio
The sound of girls giggling, feet tapping and thumping,
bars rattling, fans whirling, music playing.

The nuances of a dance studio
Cold water flowing down your throat,
quenching your thirst;
warm soda in your mouth,
cheap paper cups with wax coating
peeling off onto your lips.

The nuances of a dance studio
Rough wood of the bars, dusty floors,
old carpet flat and grimy,
worn out cushions on the rough wood bench.

THE NUANCES OF A DANCE STUDIO

Sarah Vernier

St. Teresa School
Belleville, IL
Nominated by eighth grade teacher Sharon Fahrner

Anticolor

Pale blue flower...tell me your secret.
Speak not to me in your riddles,
but in the spectrum of your glistening nectar.

Dance in the thought of my essence,
being one with you and your brilliant petals.
Sway in the melody of my blissful mood.

Breathe at last when my sullen mood
awakens you.

Sarah Diane Pikul

St. Teresa School
Belleville, IL
Nominated by eighth grade teacher Sharon Fahrner

Wonders of Winter

Evergreen trees glisten with snow,
The water has lost its rhythm and flow.
I skate with beauty, wonder, and grace
Keeping up a steady pattern and pace.
The stone fence reaches for the flakes,
As they slowly descend onto the slumbering lake.
The cold crisp wind whispers in my ear,
As I glide through air, crisp and clear.
The birds sing a tune in the bare oak tree,
A glorious melody they sound out to me.
The land is a large blanket of white,
Glistening like a beautiful light.
The lake rests under the still blue sky,
There's nothing around but winter and I.

Dayne Wittenbrink

St. John the Baptist Catholic School
Red Bud, IL
Nominated by eighth grade teacher Kristie Fahey

Pilgrimage

On Board

The hard, cruel waters beat terrifyingly
against the cold ribs of the immense ship,
days drag on like the taunts of our persecutors
in Mother Country,
deep blue seas reach for eternity
with the great white angels hovering over them,
sadness dwells in the souls
of this heavily crowded home,
depression is familiar in the hearts of many
suffering aboard this desolate contraption.

Gray skies tread the barren path of death's devastation,
bubbling foam of this black sea
welcome the many casualties of this voyage,
water is scarce beyond that flowing from our eyes,
many are worried about the voyage's end,
if there is one, mutiny is coming.
My feet, painted with grime,
touched the moist shore of the New World,
I knelt down on the sandy shore
and kissed it as waves trickled at my feet,
I was home! This was our home!

Winter

White, all white!
Snow everywhere, it goes on and on, so much snow,
horrid snow,
devastation hovers over us like the confusion
at the Tower of Babel,
the black of man's sin seems to have taken our fate,
God help us!!

Starvation is a shadow that lingers as a deep fog
reminding us of our departure from Mother Country,
we plead for God's grace and protection,
the graves get more numerous each day,
the poor souls, we pray for Your help Lord!

Hearts break daily, and the mounds of dirt keep rising,
we are flooding with tears
and indescribable pain and sorrow,
we need Your deliverance Lord,
shield us with Your hand, Lord,
and guide us with Your Holy Spirit!

Fields of Gold

The deaths are like the casualties of war,
many suffer horrid deaths in the deadly cold
of this unjust winter,
those who survived the cruel winter
were eager to start anew,
we planted many crops.

The kindness of one lone Indian saved our lost cause,
his wise council gave us the fight
we needed to survive,
I owe my life to an Indian,
God's gift, we owe our life to an Indian.

We will survive, we will live on,
we will fight to live,
thank You, God,
You alone have answered prayer,
thank You for all and
Squanto!

The Indian Way

We owe all our lives to You Lord,
the corn are sprouting
their slender deep leaves stained green,
the soil is rich and I dig my feet into its coolness,
I owe this all to You,
I'll serve You forever and live by Your rules daily,
I'm Yours!
The great kindness of the Indians has taught us
and kept us alive,
Your grace has given us the victory after the winter,
we have learned to kill prey, and fish,
we use the fish as food and to help the crops,
our killing trait taught to us by the Indians,
might be a grave trait to know,
someday we might have a war,
God forbid!

For God

You have taught us humility, patience,
and hope in You, only You,
You have inflicted on us sorrow, joy, and friendship,
we could not ask for anything more,
You have given us everlasting love, hope, guidance,
and shelter,
our lives would be nonexistent if not for You,
we serve You daily in humble servitude,
we rejoice in praise for You and honor Your holiness,
we owe everything to You,
we give thanks, praise and honor for Your
ever-loving grace,
Thank You Lord!!

Today the leaves are gold, brown, and red,
they have settled on the earth's floor,
today we give thanks for all you have done for us
this long year,
we sit now at your table, Lord, to give thanks to you,
we fellowship from your grace, giving thanks,
we give thanks to you Lord,
we love you, we owe everything to you,
we give thanks with the Indians, for you and to you,
we fellowship in perfect harmony.

A Tribute

Many may run from you, and curse your name,
but Lord you are my God and I give my all to you,
I give my life to you,
my mere existence on the face of this earth
is a gift from you,
I owe every breath I have taken to you,
I pray to you Lord to forgive my every sin,
my life in this strange,
new world would have never been without you,
I owe it all to you!
Thank you Lord for life, thank you for everything,
we honor and love YOU!!

Thank You!

Tristan Bevans

Quincy Junior High
Quincy, IL
Nominated by eighth grade teacher Deborah Birch

Tomorrow's Wishes

A glare from the sun on a pond,
Is wandering in my mind.
As I walk through the forest,
A vision I wish to find.

Above I look at the big bright sky,
And hope to see a reason why,
The stars do shine and the birds do sing,
A promise of hope they all do bring.

Whenever I feel sad or lonely,
I think of tomorrow's wishes.
They bring me happiness and so I say,
"Hurry tomorrow and good-bye today."

Kim Garkie

Quincy Junior High
Quincy, IL
Nominated by eighth grade teacher Deborah Birch

Light, Light Up Tonight

Light, light up
When I see you, your eyes sparkle
At me through your
Screen of lashes
When you see me

I wonder why
I waited so long
For you to see me
Through your long,
Long lashes.

You see me and our eyes lock
We know it's love,
But we're blind to the obstacles.
That face you and me through
The long, long night.

Jennifer Smith

Quincy Junior High
Quincy, IL
Nominated by eighth grade teacher Deborah Birch

Friendship

The world can be a wonderful place
with friends by your side.
The sort of place one finds only in
fairy tales and dreams and beaches
with ocean tides.
Or it can be a land of cool refreshing
springs and sunsets that blaze across the sky.
The friendship that we've grown on,
will never ever die.
The bond that we have is definitely strong.
Our friends have always been there
even if we were right or wrong.
They've been there to pick us up when we fell,
to comfort us when we were hurt,
and to tell us that we're O.K.
Plus telling us that they haven't got
the time or more important things to do.
But yet we don't think it's right but it comes out true.
The bond that we have will never be
broken through thick or thin.
We are a circle of friends, we have no lines,
and we have no points to end.

Christina Marie Queen

Payson-Seymour Jr. High
Payson, IL
Nominated by eighth grade teacher Janet Kroencke

Change

People change
Does that mean that I cannot change
Because I am different in color or religion?
No, it does not
I am just like you inside and out
I can run, jump, breathe the same as the
Next person
I have thoughts and rights
I can do whatever I please
No one can tell me I can't change
Because I can and I will
I can change.

Christina Mason

Payson-Seymour Jr. High
Payson, IL
Nominated by eighth grade teacher Janet Kroencke

Always

Friends are pals
They are always there
Even when no one seems to care
I will always be there, whenever you need me,
You will never have to plead.
I will be a friend always; indeed.
Friends are fun to be with.
They do things with you like shopping or school.
They even give you their time.
Sometimes they call just to say "Hi,"
Or a shoulder so you can cry,
And sometimes just to share gossip.
They like to confide their feelings
About love and boys.
Sometimes I have feelings to share,
Because friends take turns being there when needed
Because friends are there forever!

Amanda Dusenbery

Beardstown CUSD # 15
Beardstown, IL
Nominated by eighth grade teacher Colleen Martin

The best of the best
The worst of the worst;
Have you ever wondered
What is best and
What could be worse?
Sometimes maybe, maybe
Things couldn't get worse,
But they somehow do.
Sometimes things are the
Best they've ever been.
Sometimes you're on top of the ladder,
But somehow you fall off again.
Why, do you ask,
Does life throw so many
Curve balls?
Maybe, just maybe, someday
You will reach the top
Of that worn-out ladder.

Jim Shadowens

Cisne Middle School
Cisne, IL
Nominated by eighth grade teacher Linda Keck

I often wonder.
I wonder about cats.
I want to know what they look like.
If they are fat,
Or if they look like bats?
I want to know what they act like.
If they act like tykes,
Or can they ride bikes?
I want to know what they do,
And if they like their hairdos.
I want to know how long they live.
Is it,
one,
three,
six,
or even nine?
Also do they like wine?
I wonder if they like to purr?
Or like the color of their fur?
Never give your cat a whack,
Even if their fur is black.

The other day I won a bet.
So I went and bought a pet.
Wonder what I got?
Take a guess.
Her name is Bess!

Abbey Elizabeth Sabo

West Lincoln/Broadwell
Lincoln, IL
Nominated by eighth grade teacher Phillis Read

What Is Under The Couch?

I stuck my hand under the couch
And I didn't really find anything except a mouse!
But with that mouse came a beautiful house!
Tagging along was a dog that was fetching a hog!
Now on the back of the hog was an eight-foot log!
Nailed to the eight-foot log
Was a cup of molded eggnog!
On the hook of the cup was a little duck!
Stuck to the little sucker was a pacifier!
On that pacifier was some cat litter
That can be easily washed with something bitter!
No wonder the mouse ran out so quickly,
The cheese in the mousetrap was moldy and yucky!
As I continued my search under the couch
The rusty old nail gave me an OUCH!
My bloody skin and the carpet had some bondage
So I decided to put a bandage!
Hey, I found the last piece to the puzzle
Now my room will dazzle!
Found a piece to the vacuum
But now I got to go the bathroom!

Ilyas Lakada

Jamieson Elementary School
Chicago, IL
Nominated by eighth grade teacher
Demetra Antonopoulos

Poppy

Photos and stories,
memories of you.
All that I have of
a grandfather
I never knew.

Born in 1912.
Lived through the Great Depression.
Lost his parents at the
tender age of five.
Yet still he lived his life
giving
first to his country;
later to his family.

Raised seven children
on fifteen grand a year.
His courage and generosity
makes me swell with pride.

I wish you were living still
so I could hold you near.
To learn from and talk to,
the grandpa I hold dear.

A tribute to Robert Pierce

Meghan Pierce

Ebinger
Chicago, IL
Nominated by eighth grade teacher Jessica Chethik

Hockey
a slushy sheet of ice,
a wooden stick and rubber puck,
I curve, I skate, I swerve,
I skate to a whirring sound,
I can go fast or go slow,
But, I always go for the goal,
Everybody skates to win,
Before the time comes to an end.

Jason Hayden

Our Lady Queen of Peace School
Belleville, IL
Nominated by eighth grade teacher Rosemary Buss

Friends

Friends are people who care about you
Through good times and bad times and all
through your life

Friends make you laugh and do many fun things
Throughout your friendship your feelings never change

Friends are always right by your side
Through rumors and fights and many hard times

Friends are there through thick and thin
You feel so lucky you have such great friends

Even though you get into fights
In the end it turns out all right

It's nice to know you have such great friends
To talk to and hang with until the end

Then when it comes you know you'll meet again
Right up in Heaven with the Lord and His friends

Paul DeVito

B.V.M. Help of Christians
Woodside, NY
Nominated by eighth grade teacher
Sheila Smith-Gonzalez

Wrapped In Liberty

As others cover
themselves,
to protect themselves,
from the cold,
men and women wrap
a word around themselves,
liberty,
killing and looting,
all in the name
of liberty,
surrounded by their
armor,
their reason,
why the killing is
all right,
why children can
become orphans
why families should
starve
all for the sake of
liberty,
whose?
who sees the destruction and
continues,
a blind eye is turned,
excuses made,
the end justifies the means,
no one means death,
but death it becomes,

a young boy asked by a man in uniform what liberty is,
answering the truth,
the reason I am alone,
why my village is gone,
liberty means death to many,
too many?
the blanket is raised,
covering the eyes,
no cry can be heard,
for liberty resounds,
no mind can believe,
a dream is secured,
no death can dislodge it,
all the glory of a crippled man,
a purple heart
is awarded,
to mask the reality,
an honor is bestowed,
to the man blinded it matters not.
The shrill cry,
Liberty,
for one and all,
and the dead,
an unheard voice whispers.

Hanina Stettin

Maimonides Academy
Los Angeles, CA
Nominated by eighth grade teacher N. Chodos

Running From You
(Drugs)

I came running gracefully
To find a creature almost like me.

I saw a flash of orange out of
the corner of my eye.
The flash of orange froze
the poor creature's mind.

I heard the pounding of the heart
from the orange blot,
Suddenly I heard a loud gunshot.

I saw the soft smoke which
took the shape of a blimp.
I looked over to see the poor creature go limp.

Now I am running from you for
I do not know what to do.

But when the long narrow black strip
is pointed at me.
You will see me run faster than a laser beam.

Ashley Alexander

Hanover-Horton Middle
Horton, MI
Nominated by eighth grade teacher Deda Clark

Drop Of Water

I'm falling, falling, falling
from the big, gray cloud
Lightning crashes to the world
Its thunderous boom is loud.

I'm falling, falling, falling
through the dark, night sky
The cold wind whistles right on by me
It almost sounds like a sweet lullaby.

I'm falling, falling, falling
almost to the ground
I keep thinking of my arrival
Hopefully, safe and sound.

I'm falling, falling, falling
trying to land on someone fat
But then they moved right out of my way
And I heard a loud Ka-Splat.

Ian Erdmann

Franklin Monroe MS/HS
Pitsburg, OH
Nominated by eighth grade teacher Sherri Leasure

My Wings

I perish
I fail
I fall
I stagger
My wings are folded
I fade
I stumble
I scream
I cry
My wings begin to spread
I proceed
I persist
I strengthen
I rise
My wings will lift me up
I persevere
I bloom
I flourish
I triumph
My wings will make me fly

Susan Retterbush

Franklin Monroe MS/HS
Pitsburg, OH
Nominated by eighth grade teacher Sherri Leasure

I Am Young; You Are Old

I am water, and you are fire.
I am white, and you are black.
I am innocent, and you are guilty.
I am inexperienced, and you are wise.
I am strong, and you are weak.
I am rich, and you are poor.
I am satisfied, and you are hungry.
I am a soldier, and you are a veteran.
I am young, and you are old.

But we live in society where

the water diminishes the flames,
the black and white mingle to form gray,
the innocent guide the guilty,
the inexperienced learn from the wise,
the strong help the weak,
the rich aid the poor,
the satisfied feed the hungry,
the veteran teaches the soldier,

and

the young soon become old.

Laura Fuller

Franklin Monroe MS/HS
Pitsburg, OH
Nominated by eighth grade teacher Sherri Leasure